D1717232

OFF ROAD VEHICLES
DUNE BUGGIES

KENNY ABDO

abdopublishing.com

Published by Abdo Zoom, a division of ABDO, P.O. Box 398166, Minneapolis, Minnesota 55439. Copyright © 2018 by Abdo Consulting Group, Inc. International copyrights reserved in all countries. No part of this book may be reproduced in any form without written permission from the publisher.

Printed in the United States of America, North Mankato, Minnesota.
092017
012018

Photo Credits: Alamy, iStock, Shutterstock
Production Contributors: Kenny Abdo, Jennie Forsberg, Grace Hansen
Design Contributors: Dorothy Toth, Neil Klinepier

Publisher's Cataloging-in-Publication Data

Names: Abdo, Kenny, author.
Title: Dune buggies / by Kenny Abdo.
Description: Minneapolis, Minnesota: Abdo Zoom, 2018. | Series: Off road vehicles
    Includes online resource and index.
Identifiers: LCCN 2017939273 | ISBN 9781532121012 (lib.bdg.)
    ISBN 9781532122132 (ebook) | ISBN 9781532122699 (Read-to-Me ebook)
Subjects: LCSH: Dune Buggy--Juvenile literature. | Vehicles--Juvenile literature.
    Motor Sports--Juvenile literature.
Classification: DDC 629.222--dc23
LC record available at https://lccn.loc.gov/2017939273

TABLE OF CONTENTS

DUNE BUGGIES

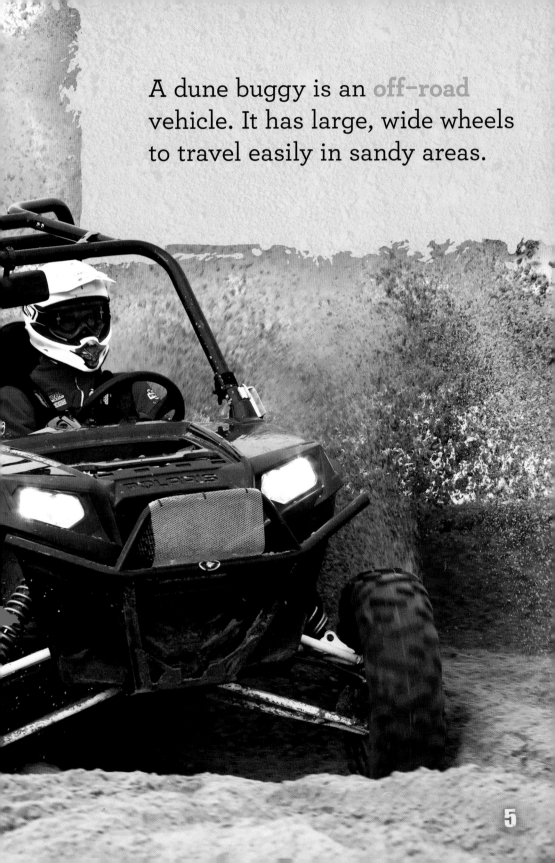

A dune buggy is an off-road vehicle. It has large, wide wheels to travel easily in sandy areas.

Dune buggies are used to drive on dunes, beaches, deserts, and more!

TYPES

Beachgoers would strip down smaller cars and put off-road tires on them. This is how dune buggies were created.

Dune buggy frames can be made from fiberglass. They are also made from tube-frames.

Tube-frames are mostly used for non-racing dune buggies. They can be driven on all types of terrain.

Special dune buggies are used by the **military**. Those are called Light Strike Vehicles (LSVs).

There are also swamp buggies. They are used in swampy areas. Swamp buggy racing is a popular pastime in the southern United States.

Drivers will race dune buggies. Sometimes it is for sport and sometimes it is for fun.

Some dune buggies are street legal and can be driven anywhere. Some buggies are not and must be **towed** by a truck.

GLOSSARY

dune – a hill or ridge of loose sand piled up by the wind.

fiberglass – a material made of plastic and very fine fibers of glass.

military – a country's armed forces.

off-road – riding a vehicle on difficult roads or tracks, like sand, mud, or gravel.

stripped-down – a vehicle reduced to basics.

terrain – a piece of land having certain features.

tow – to pull a vehicle along with a rope or chain.

ONLINE RESOURCES

Booklinks
NONFICTION NETWORK
FREE! ONLINE NONFICTION RESOURCES

To learn more about dune buggies, please visit abdobooklinks.com. These links are routinely monitored and updated to provide the most current information available.

INDEX